This book is written with special thanks to Karen, my loving wife and best friend, and my three kids; Connor, Patrick & Olivia, who give me faith every day that the world actually does have great things ahead of it!

Michael

Table of Contents

Introduction

"Life has an odd way of making things work out in the end."

If someone rang a bell at exactly the worst time to enter the financial advisory profession, I must have heard it ring. Want to be convinced? What if I told you the markets were lower 10 years after I started than when I began. Yeah, that kind of bad timing.

My formative teen years were during the 1980's, the testosterone-filled decade of Ronald Reagan, the fall of the Berlin Wall ending the Cold War and the movie *Wall Street* where Michael Douglas's character, Gordon Gecko, claims "Greed is Good!" That was followed by the stock market rocket ship straight up through the 1990's, fueled by all the new technology companies' Initial Public Offerings (IPOs) daily that would double and triple in price overnight. As the late 1990's rolled around and I had toiled away as a Financial Officer for a small family business for seven years after college, the business was sold, and I felt that I was missing out and needed a seat on Wall Street's rocket. I was going to be the next Gordon Gecko.

In 2000, I traded my blue-collar stable-pay-check to find my fortunes buying and selling investments at a national brokerage firm. During the initial months of training, the markets continued to rise. I could hardly wait to pass the securities exam so I could be unleashed and make my mark. Well, a funny thing happened on the way to that "mark." From 2000-2002, the US stock markets crashed to the tune of nearly 50%!

What I found was that, in my naivete where I was thinking that my newly-minted role as a Financial Advisor was to get people the maximum return on their money, as I sat around countless kitchen tables with husbands and wives devastated by the stock markets crash, the conversations we were having were about how they could no longer afford to retire. The money they had in mutual funds for their kids' college was wiped out, and what they wanted to know was, "How could this happen?" What I also found is that when people have lost a significant portion of their life's savings, they were like deer in the headlights and would not make any decisions, including investing decisions. That doesn't bode well for a broker's compensation.

How the Financial Crash Busted My Own Plans

That aforementioned Gordon Gecko success story that never happened turned into several years of pinching pennies, bologna sandwiches and come-to-Jesus moments when I spun on whether had I made the right choice not only for a career, but for the financial stability of my young family, which included Karen, my wife, and at the time, two children, Connor, 2, and Patrick, 1. There were numerous nights where I would ask, "Is this really worth it?" The financial hardship on my family escalated, with my income being half of what we were making before, combined with a new strain on my marriage due to mounting financial obligations while trying to balance young kids. Amazingly, Karen's support and personal belief in me and my career decision never waivered, even if internally it did.

The one moment that it almost fell apart and I was about to call "Uncle" was on Christmas Eve, 2001. I had a surprisingly good November, and I was paid three weeks after the close of the last month. Karen and I didn't have the money to buy Christmas gifts for the kids because our bank account was coasting on fumes from a rocky year in the markets and by clients paralyzed with inaction.

The great news was that everything was soon to be history, as the check was about to arrive in the mail which was going to solve all our financial ills. The postman came, I dashed to the mailbox, probably had bugs in my teeth as I was smiling all the way to it. "This is it...this is what all the struggle was for!" That's all I could think. As I walked back towards the house, with Karen waiting on the front porch stoop, I ripped open the pay envelope and as quickly as the excitement came to me when I had heard the postal Jeep coming down my street, there was an immediate pit that dropped into my stomach. The check was for $26.54. Nope, that's not a typo. What I had expected to be a $6,000 check was $26.54 on Christmas Eve. It would be a dollar store Christmas.

Come to figure that in my low production months, the firm was holding back and passing on operating costs to me like licensing, marketing and overhead.

Unbeknownst to me, this would be the time that they chose to call in their chips for those expenses. I felt exactly like the countless clients with whom I had been speaking. I recalled all the conversations of "We did the right thing, worked hard, kept plugging away to finally get ahead and then had it all taken away from us at the time we needed it the most." That was me on Christmas Eve.

Lessons Learned That Now Benefit My Clients

I couldn't even look at Karen and walked past her in shame, then went straight to the bedroom at first in shock, then later in personal disappointment. I knew at that moment I needed to make a choice. Either I had to leave the financial industry for the financial health of my family and marriage or I had to be better and never again put my family and my clients in a situation where they felt financially helpless. Thankfully, in retrospect, I took the path that has provided financial success for my clients and my family for nearly two decades.

Those candid kitchen table conversations were formative in how I approached every client relationship going forward and still do to this day. As if it were a smack to the head where life told me to "wake up," I realized that my true life's calling as a Financial Advisor was not to maximize the returns for my clients at any cost and espouse the virtues of performance. My value as an advisor was to dig deeper and protect my clients from all the things that could go wrong which might derail their financial plan. This is the idea of assigning a Purpose to our financial plan, which we can control, rather than just chasing Performance that we have no control over.

Unfortunately, the industry and Wall Street's business model didn't change after the 2000-2002 bear market. The industry, even today, seems more aligned with squeezing every fee imaginable out of everyday investors and providing little-to-no customer service or hand-holding in the process.

Ultimate Answer Lay With My Own Firm

For those reasons, in 2008, I broke away from a traditional Wall Street investment bank and founded my own independent financial planning firm, Crystal Lake Tax & Financial. The Mission is simple: we want to be all things financial planning for our clients. Anything you can do with money, we can assist our clients with, including conservative financial planning, tax preparation and estate planning. While providing these services, it's in a cost-effective manner with an emphasis on personal service and regular communication. We operate as a Fiduciary in all our engagements, which means for our investment advisory business, we are fee-based (not commissions) and beholden by law to act in the best interest of our clients, for their benefit, not ours. Holistic, comprehensive financial planning and investment management that is goals-based and touches every aspect of our clients' lives is our marching order.

After 18 years as a financial advisor and navigating our clients through two bear markets, where the stock markets have declined 50% or more twice, our value continues to be in coaching clients on the steps required to define and achieve their personal financial goals and avoid the common financial landmines and red flags that can do financial harm.

In the chapters ahead, I will cover many of these financial lessons learned and how to avoid the landmines on your journey to enjoying a successful retirement with independence and dignity.

Purpose vs. Performance

"You can be young without money, but you can't be old without it."

-Tennessee Williams

When it comes to investing, there are many landmines, myths and obstacles for investors, some of which we will cover in subsequent chapters. In this initial chapter, I seek to address the idea of investing for a Purpose, compared to strictly for Performance. Having the ability to understand this concept will play a large factor in achieving your family's financial goals.

People think they need to invest to keep pace with what the markets or other investors are doing, rather than taking a step back and realizing what I call "The Economy of You," which is what rate of return do you need to achieve all of your family's financial goals. Then, based on that real-world rate of return, determine how much risk you should or should not be taking. This approach takes all the concerns away from focusing on performance and defines success as achieving the true purpose of why you are investing: to provide a retirement income you can't outlive and perhaps spend time with the grandkids, volunteer, and give back. If you can achieve all of your financial goals over time while reducing stress simultaneously, isn't that an ideal outcome?

The Wall Street marketing machine continues its Performance-driven siren song forever, luring individual investors to crash at the banks of performance, causing their financial demise. In their advertisements, they highlight star rankings of mutual funds and recent quarterly performance, as if either of those things are tied into a lifetime financial plan. The business of Wall Street is not to make clients' money, but rather to get them to buy something.

Consider the brokerage and mutual fund business model itself. Many are publicly traded, all are for-profit organizations, and their duty is to maximize shareholder value. Note that their obligation is not to make you money. Your ownership of their fund is their means to an end – profits - regardless of whether you make money or not. How do they accomplish this? By charging high internal fees and marketing to the public to attract more assets that they alone have the better mousetrap style of investing. In reality, that is just marketing rhetoric, and study after study shows most actively managed stock funds underperform the very stock market indexes against which they are benchmarked.

There must be a better way. In fact, there is. Let me explain.

How Investing for Purpose Delivers on Client Goals

The investing philosophy we have used as the guide for our clients for nearly two decades has been one of investing for Purpose, not Performance. Investing for Purpose is an approach where we are investing to achieve specific tangible goals and to take only the reasonable risk necessary to be successful to achieve those goals, regardless of short-term market conditions.

A problem with most financial advisors is that they actually serve less as an advisor and pretend to be more of a portfolio manager. They tout that their selection of mutual funds will beat some other guy's mutual funds in performance. Why this fails is for two reasons: 1) the selection of the investments are not tied to specific goals and 2) performance is not something that can be controlled. The relationship with the client then becomes one of solely performance: "Am I up or am I down...How did my funds do this quarter?" That is shortsighted, as no one can control the markets, but what we can control is our anticipated rate of return, how much risk we are taking and have an understanding of why we are invested in a specific manner. That pulls it all together where the goals drive the portfolio composition, not the uncontrollable market. Portfolio management is a part of the advisory relationship, but should not be the only part of an advisory relationship.

A True Advisory Relationship is Tailored to Your Needs

How should your advisory relationship look? The conversation shouldn't be about market returns and market outlooks or even about fees, rather it should be a genuine conversation covering:

- o What do you need this money to do for you and your family?
- o How do you plan to provide for a retirement that could last through three decades?
- o How confident are you that your income will be sufficient to maintain your quality of life throughout retirement?
- o How do you feel about the level of risk you're taking? Do you know how much risk you're taking? (most don't)

These questions may sound like common sense matters to address, but so many advisors just don't ask.

Common sense isn't common practice.

The other brokers wish to be aspiring portfolio managers and don't want to spend time talking with you regarding what's important about money to you, ways to lower your taxes now and in retirement, showing you in black and white today how your future retirement income is locked in, and assisting with estate planning to ensure you leave the legacy you want. Essentially, the advisor should advise on all matters financial.

From the feedback I've received while helping hundreds of retirees over the past two decades, the typical broker conversation goes something like, "You've got money to invest? Let me pull out a brochure of a recently good performing mutual fund mix, sign here, and you can just write a check to ABC Financial Firm. Oh, and don't expect any level of service or your phone to ring." Of course, I'm being a bit wry, but that's how they say it feels.

A true advisory conversation about your retirement and retirement income should go more like the following;

"Today, we will do two things. The first thing is to sit together and talk through what retirement looks like for you and the retirement income we are going to need to maintain the quality of life you want and deserve while retired. The second thing is to create a detailed financial plan that will analyze all the sources of retirement income available and compare those to your projected living expenses in retirement. If we're fine, then we may need only tweaks. If we come to a point that it looks like you may not be able to achieve that level of income without some changes, then we have some decisions to make.

This is not a rushed process, and I have no investment recommendations for you. In fact, it would be malpractice to offer an investment when we aren't even sure yet what you need to achieve your goals. This process will take 3-4 meetings, but you will leave with an understanding of exactly where you are and what needs to be done to ensure the retirement lifestyle you deserve."

The Long-Term Strategy is Where the Gold Lies

Can you see the difference between an advisor wannabe who is more interested in getting the sale and using short-term performance as the reason compared to a true advisor that attempts to work alongside you and guide you down the path of a successful retirement plan based on your specific goals - a Purpose?

In many conversations with clients, they felt they were "sold" something when they began working with their former advisors. There was no discussion on hopes, wants and goals. Folks, investing is only about achieving hopes, wants and goals. If we are investing purely for the thrill of performance, then it's just gambling. The one thing we know about is performance-based investing, with gains not taken potentially becoming losses.

The reason I emphasize retirement income so much is that we are taught by Wall Street marketing and commercials that the goal of investing is to accumulate more and more. The drum beat of "Invest for growth...Time in the market, not timing the market" goes on and on, regardless of market conditions. The reality is that we don't need "principal" in retirement, we need income. When you're in retirement, you won't put gas in the car with principal. If you go golfing in retirement, you won't spend principal. When you take the grandkids on vacation to Disney World, you don't spend principal. In all these examples, you want to spend "income" - dividends and interest. The last thing you want to do in retirement is spend down principal. That's how you end up running out of money before you run out of life.

How to Shape a Retirement Income Plan

A solid retirement income plan must focus on two areas. The first is retirement income that you cannot outlive, regardless of market conditions or interest rates. The second is a retirement income that can grow at least at the cost of living for the balance of both you and your spouse's lives.

So how do you determine the rate of return, with the least amount of risk, that you need to achieve a lifetime of income while considering the need for a rising income over time to keep up with the cost of living?

When you consider the boom and bust cycles since 2000[i] where the S&P 500 made money heading in to 2000, lost nearly half during 2000-2002, returned to close to even in 2007, only to see it decline close to half 2007-2009, then went back to even in 2013 and added additional gains to reach new highs, it stands to reason that the market appears to go up more than down. But when it declines, it tends to decline faster than it rose. I joke with clients that the market takes the stairs up (slow) and the elevator down (fast). To recap the past nearly two decades of market history, the cycle goes...Made It, Lost It, Made It, Lost It, Made It...and here we are.

Countless prospective clients have sat at my office conference table after a significant downturn in the stock markets, stating that greed got the best of them. They knew they were taking too much risk or that their broker told them to just "hang on" and it all ended badly. They had gains, until they didn't. This is the FOMO (Fear of Missing Out) that guides clients who worry about missing out on the next 5 to 10% of the upside of the market. Knowingly or not, they risk losses of -20% or more. You don't believe me? Think about the two bear markets we've had in the last 20 years wiping out half of all market value each time.[ii]

The Downside of Market Timing

As an investor, your goal is not to meet or achieve all the upside of the stock market and try to time the next downturn to get out. Timing and Selection of market entry points is not investing, it's a fool's game, it's gambling. You win, until you don't.

I will share with you an exercise I take new clients through on the whiteboard in my office when trying to determine the amount of portfolio risk they should take. I write the following: $TR = I + G(L)$. To those who haven't been blessed to witness my marker skills, I will walk you through what that equation means (and I promise to limit math speak).

$$TR = I + G(L)$$

"TR" represents Total Return. It answers what is the acceptable rate of return we are planning for over the next five or more years? By knowing the Total Return that is anticipated, then we can (based on historical asset class return assumptions) determine how much risk is acceptable and the sources of potential return.

"I" represents income, which is interest and dividends from our income-generating investments (e.g. bonds, bond-like instruments, preferred stocks, REITs). Essentially the "I" represents holdings that produce regular income payments every month or quarter, regardless of the principal fluctuation based on the claims-paying ability of the issuer.

"G" represents growth, most likely capital gain and appreciation from stock market-based investments (e.g. stocks, stock mutual funds, index funds) that are more speculative. The problem with "G" (Growth) is that it can become "L" (Losses), and diminishes Total Return. A big enough "L" can wipe out years of "G," right at the time we are in or nearing retirement, thus potentially wreaking financial havoc at the most inopportune time.

Here's a hypothetical example: if a client is comfortable with a 7% total return over time (not any given year, but an average over time), then their equation looks like 7% = I + G. Now let's take that a step further, what if we could get income and dividends of about 5% in the "I" bucket. Now our equation looks like 7% = 5% + G. Think to yourself, how much additional return do we need from G (Growth) to achieve the expected rate of return? The answer is a much smaller amount and less market risk than most are currently taking.

Unfortunately, many advisors have their clients predominately in G, with hope as a strategy. When markets turn, who gets hurt, the broker? No, you. Did you get to keep the gains? Alas, no. Gains not taken may become losses.

Managing Your Returns as Retirement Approaches

If you're in retirement, or less than 10 years from retirement, this is the concept of managing to the return you need to achieve to reach your household financial goals - your Purpose.

Equally as importantly, at this stage in your life, with the market seemingly setting new highs daily, what strategy are you implementing to not try and beat the market to address your FOMO, but rather protect the substantial assets you've saved over a lifetime? Money should be managed to achieve your goals, not to keep up with some arbitrary index.

So, what's the underlying lesson from this chapter? The lesson is that your retirement is your retirement alone. The advice you follow and the investments that you make must be dictated 100% by your Purpose and seek only answers to two criteria:

First, am I positioned to provide enough income for the rest of our lives, independent of market conditions?

Second, having confidence to answer 1, am I positioned for a rising income to keep up with the cost of living?

If you're not sure, or worse yet, know the answers are "No," then you need to sit down with a true retirement income planner and avoid financial sales people who lead with performance, like a plague that can cause you serious financial harm.

Bonus item...How to determine immediately if you are in front of a Financial Salesperson

Answer: If an investment product is recommended in the first meeting, before understanding all your overall financial needs and concerns, then you are in the lion's den. Deliver a "Thank you for your time" and scoot out of there. In that instance, we know who is getting taken care of, and you're not on the list.

Eat the Eggs, Not the Chickens

"Retirement is like a long vacation in Las Vegas. The goal is to enjoy it the fullest, but not so fully that you run out of money."

-Jonathan Clements

One of the most important benefits I offer as an independent financial advisor is educating clients and prospective clients about some of the myths, fallacies and half-truths that Wall Street puts out as propaganda to influence investor behavior for its benefit, not the clients'.

Let me ask you a critical question: If you had enough income in retirement to do all the things you wanted to do, would you care about account balances or market ups and downs? No, it's all about generating income. In retirement, growth is important, but it is secondary to a reliable income generating portfolio. Keep that answer in mind as you study this chapter and see how the investment advice you need to be successful in retirement isn't what you've been getting from Wall Street brokerage firms.

In my nearly two decades of experience, I've found that many people have done an excellent job at saving for retirement, but what they haven't done is translate that into specific goals for retirement, including how much retirement income they will need and how they will generate it.

My role when sitting down with clients is to identify not only their goals, but any red flags that may cause them financial harm. What I often see, after clients have defined their goals, is that the strategies they are using are in direct conflict with their goals. In most instances, they are taking too much risk, paying too much in fees and have no real plan for retirement income. All of these factors can cause financial harm. We know your 401k can become a 201k overnight and drop by half. It's happened two times in the last 17 years. It's not a matter of *if* it's going to happen, it's a matter of *when*.

Planning for Surprises

What would you do if the market dropped by -30%? What's your Plan B? Do you have a Plan B? The default Plan B for many is to work longer, take less income and wait years for the market to recover.

I am a big believer in common sense solutions. My experience has shown that the more complicated something is, the greater the likelihood is that I'm getting taken advantage of. In investing, I tend to be more "old fashioned," meaning, when I need income, I need to live off the interest and not spend the principal.

Live Off the Interest, Don't Spend Principal

Do you remember your parents and grandparents talking about that? I do.

Let me share an analogy I give clients: consider that your principal is your collection of chickens and the chickens lay eggs regularly. The eggs represent interest and dividends. As long as we have chickens, then we will always get our eggs (steady income). What happens if we eat the chickens? Then the eggs go away and eventually we don't have chickens or eggs. Bringing this full circle, if we need income, eat the eggs, don't eat the chickens. Seems like good old common sense. Unfortunately, too many advisors are telling clients that the way to generate retirement income is to pray the market goes up and start eating chickens (selling shares to create income). This is a strategy that can end in financial disaster and cause you to run out of money. Remember, eat the eggs (interest) not the chickens (principal).

When did that concept change, to live off the interest? When Wall Street realized that they could make more money keeping you invested rather than protecting what you have. The idea of "Buy and Hold" as a mainstream mantra came into existence from 1982 and onward, and it was never an investment strategy until Wall Street flipped the script.

Do you hear anyone talking about that today...live off the interest, don't spend the principal? No. Do you know why? Most of the brokers got in to financial services in the last 30 years, and they drank- the Wall Street Kool-Aid. If markets drop -20% or -30%, what's your broker going to tell you? "Buy & Hold...Don't time the market...Stay the course." After all, it's not their money, and they've been brainwashed.

Proper Use of History's Lessons

With the best bull market in history occurring between 1987-2000[iii], many brokers and individual investors can fall prey to what in psychology is called "normalcy bias." Normalcy bias states that our early and recent experiences form our current thoughts.[iv] If things were great when we were trained, they will always be great. If things have been great during the last few years, then they will be great going forward. Basically, what is normal today, will be normal tomorrow. Bad things won't happen to me. This is why we are doomed to repeat the mistakes of the past and think "This time is different." Whether it's the South Sea Bubble, Tulip Bulb Mania, 1920's stock boom, Tech Wreck in 2000, Mortgage Meltdown 2007 or Bitcoin in 2017, normalcy bias makes us forget the mistakes of the past. Part of my job is to see through any normalcy bias you may have.

When most of these brokers were trained, during either the 1980's or '90's, if they are financial old timers or trained after 2010 and they are newbies, they were trained in times when the market only went up. No matter what happens in the world, they automatically regurgitate "Buy & Hold...Don't time the market...Stay the course," since that's what has been beaten into their brains during training.

Let me share some stock market history, as a student of its lessons. Most brokers, if you asked them about stock market history, will only be able to tell you "it goes up over time" and "look at this 100 year chart." I, on the other hand, have studied the movement and cycles of the markets and how they may impact my clients. Those who ignore history are doomed to repeat it.

When you hear about what the average return of the market is *over time,* many would say "around 10%." If you break it down over the last 120 years, that 10% average can be broken down into two types of returns: "dividends" which are income payments and "capital gains," which is market growth. Over the last 120 years, about 3% of the returns have been from dividends and 7% from growth.[v]

Would you be surprised to know that in order to get that 7% capital gain on average, there were short periods of time when you earned double digit returns and even longer stretches that you earned 0%? So, when your broker says, hang in there for the "long term," he/she is essentially talking about what are close to 35 year secular cycles of short periods of high returns and long periods of no returns (or recovery). The chart below shows when the market has had these stretches.[vi]

10% Average Annual Returns

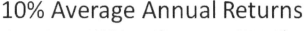

7% Growth   + 3% Dividends

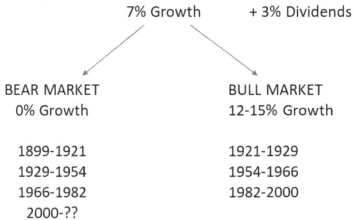

BEAR MARKET	BULL MARKET
0% Growth	12-15% Growth
1899-1921	1921-1929
1929-1954	1954-1966
1966-1982	1982-2000
2000-??	

How to read the chart:

1899-1921 The markets were flat, they went up and down but after nearly 22 years, the index was where it started.

1921-1929 You had the Roaring 20's, the invention of the mass-produced automobiles and it was a great time to be in the market.

1929-1954 The Great Depression and World War II, where it took nearly 25 years for the index to return in 1954 to where it was in 1929.

1954-1966 You had the baby boomers growing up, suburban expansion and the Nifty 50 stocks (e.g. Kodak, Avon, Polaroid, Sears, Xerox), it was a great time to be in the market.

1966-1982 The Vietnam War, sky-high interest rates, high inflation and fuel shortages. The Dow Jones Industrial Average was 1000 in 1966 and 16 years later, in 1982, it hit 1000 again.

1982-2000 This was the greatest bull market in history, Ronald Reagan, fall of the Berlin Wall, collapse of the Soviet Union, technology advancements, record Initial Public Offerings and day trading millionaires, it was a great time to be in the market.

2000-2002 The market dropped over -50% and the index did not recover until 2007.

2007-2009 We all know what happened in 2007, just as the markets broke even from seven years prior, the financial crisis, Great Recession and mortgage meltdown, where the markets tumbled again resulting in over -50% losses. Fears of another Great Depression were realistic, and the Fed cut interest rates to zero and bailed out major banks. A truly fearful time in our nation's history.

2000-2013 The market did not return to the 2000 level until 2013. You had essentially 13 years when the market was flat. Sure, it went up, crashed, went up, crashed, went up, and had you been sitting in an index fund in January 2000, you likely would have had the same amount of money 13 years later. All along, you could hear what Wall Street's brokers were saying, "Buy and Hold...Don't time the market...Stay the course." The problem is that you would have wasted one of the most valuable assets you have - your time - which is 13 years of your investing life to get back to even. Now that you're 10 years older than you were in 2008, can you afford another large market decline and wait years to break even?

2000-2017 You can't turn on the news without hearing about the markets seemingly hitting new highs daily. That's exciting to the short-term performance driven investor, and brokers will point to that. What they will tell you is that from January 2000 - December 2017, the S&P 500 went from 1320 to 2673[vii], doubling over 17 years. What they won't tell you is that the average rate of return with dividends invested for that 17 years is about 6%, not the expected 10%. Was it worth the ride of the last 17 years and the pain of two bear markets to average 6%? And that 6% does not factor in inflation.

The Way "Buy and Hold" Can Hurt You

As noted above, when Wall Street talks about the long term, when you combine the two cycles (short periods of good and long periods of flat-to-negative returns), they are talking about 35-year secular cycles to get the "average" market return. I don't know about you, but my clients live in the real world and need real returns in retirement to pay their bills, and they can't just rely on a chart that says if they stick it out for up to 35 years, then they might be OK.

Buy and hold looks great on paper, but my clients don't eat paper.

Buy and hold also doesn't take your life stage into account. If you're 20-30 years old, stay aggressive. If you're 50-60+, that mountain chart of 100 years no longer applies to you. Your investment strategy needs to be one that protects your hard-earned money and generates a rising income you cannot outlive. You need to invest for Purpose over chasing Performance.

The biggest challenge for you, if you have stock market-based portfolios as you are in or nearing retirement, is not only that you may be in or about to enter a significant period of decline (markets haven't had a significant correction in nearly a decade), but there is also the matter of how you are going to generate income in a down market. If you need 5% income, and you are in a stock based account that is down -10%, then your portfolio will drop in value -15% (your 5% income taken if you had to sell shares to get it, plus a -10% decline in market value).

Now, going into the next year, you have 85% of what you had the year prior, but you still need 5% income from the original 100%, so now you're taking a larger percentage out, plus or minus whatever the market offers in returns that next year. This is how clients run out of money - they take a little and the market takes more.

Speculative Advice to Avoid

Is there a "Re-do" button in retirement? You have to be careful. Please hear me, of all the things you take away, do not be in a position to need to sell investments (principal) for income! There is no re-do.

Your broker is making three deadly and dangerous speculations when he/she has you sell investments (eat the chickens) for income. These dangerous speculations are:

1) Your account value will be higher in the future. (over which he/she has no control)

2) You will be able to take a "projected" (think: a guess) income in the future.
3) You won't run out of money.

None of these three considerations can be assured without a true income strategy that isn't reliant on crossing your fingers, ignoring market history or dependent on stock market returns.

Going back to our Stock Market History, if you were to speak to the collective wisdom of the generation from 1929-1954 or 1966-1982 who were nearing retirement, knowing what you know now, and you told them you are either in retirement or within 10 years of retirement and you were 50%, 60% or 70% "in the market," what do you think they would tell you? I think they'd tell you that you need to protect the chickens and just eat the eggs. They lived through a decade or more of markets with little to no returns right at the time their families needed access to these funds to generate retirement income.

What do you think your broker would tell you? Buy and Hold...Don't time the market...Stay the course. He or she would point to a 100-year mountain chart of markets going up, but will gloss over the horrific financial impact it would mean if you needed income from your accounts during one of the long stretches of no or low growth.

Your parents' and grandparents' generations learned an important lesson: protect the principal and live on the interest.

Unfortunately, Wall Street has trained you to do three things:

1. Buy and hold (Why? They don't make fees if you go to cash or get conservative)
2. Teaches you to be OK doing nothing (Stay the course, we'll ride this out and collect fees along the way)

3. Teaches you to be OK with your broker doing nothing (How? With most accounts, we see the broker charging a 1.0%-1.5% Management Fee, but then they are investing in mutual funds that are actually managing the money for another 1% fee. Clients are paying 2-3% to have a mutual fund manage their money. What's the broker doing to earn their 1.5% if the mutual fund is doing all the work?)

Remember to Eat the Eggs, Not the Chickens

Going back to generating retirement income, do you pay for retirement goals with income or by selling investments (principal)? Goals are paid for by income, not principal. When you pay for goods with principal, you risk running out of money. Eat the eggs, not the chickens.

How sad is it that you've worked 90,000 hours, invested for up to 40 years, to get here, and if the market crashes, your broker is going to ask you to waste your most valuable asset -time -waiting to get back to even. It doesn't need to be this way. You've worked 90,000 hours to get to where you are today - there is no re-do. You must be careful.

Let me once again ask you a critical question: if you had enough income in retirement to do all the things you wanted to do, would you care about account balances or market ups and downs? No, it's all about generating income. In retirement, growth is important, but it is secondary to a reliable income that you and your spouse cannot outlive.

There is No Nostradamus

"Uncertainty is the only certainty there is, and knowing how to live with insecurity is the only security." --John Allen Paulos

Imagine a TV network dedicated to fortune telling. Every day, it features highly educated people who strongly believe they can predict the future. Like Isaiah, they offer their prophecy for free. Unlike Isaiah, these seers are wrong about 80% of the time. Yet, despite the failures, viewers continue to watch. Even worse, many stake their entire personal fortunes on the advice.

Would you watch such a network? Millions do. In fact, there isn't just one such channel, but two: Fox Business Channel and CNBC.

Go ahead...turn them on, especially around noon on a weekday. These channels bring on one market "expert" after another to give out stock tips or some insight as to where the market is headed.

Here's a little reality: No one...and we mean no one...knows where investment markets are headed in the next week, month, or year. If they did know, they certainly wouldn't tell you for free. In fact, they wouldn't tell you at all because such information would be far too valuable to even sell.

Remember the rule of transitive properties from Mrs. Cheeseman's math class (more on her in a minute). If A is greater than B...and B is greater than C, then A is also greater than C. Or to put it another way, if Bill is taller than Mike, and Mike is taller than Jim, then Bill is also taller than Jim. Got it?

Okay...now pay very close attention.

Markets react to news. Do you agree? Every time stocks drop in price, isn't there always some news event attributed to it (9/11,

Microsoft anti-trust suit, the Fed raising interest rates, earnings reports lower than expected)?

News is unpredictable. Do you agree? Did you know any of the following events would happen before they actually occurred?

1. Hijacked airplanes crashing into the World Trade Center and the Pentagon.
2. The Kennedy Assassination.
3. The announcement of Toxic Asset Relief Program.
4. Arthur Anderson's false accounting of Enron.
5. Pearl Harbor (okay...this one isn't fair. You probably weren't alive).

In response to each of these news events, equity markets dropped rapidly. If you did know about these events a week before they actually occurred, you could have made billions of dollars.

Two movies come to mind that demonstrate this reality.

Casino Royale (2006): James Bond seeks to defeat a card playing terrorist who makes huge rates of return by shorting stocks on companies and then staging acts of sabotage on those corporations because he knows it will drive down their stock price. In other words, he knows the news before anyone else because he's creating it.

Wall Street (1987): Gordon Gekko hires aspiring trader Bud Fox to "stop sending me information and start bringing me some." So, Bud breaks into offices at night, spies on company executives, and relays insider information told to him by his father. As a result, Gekko has "news" that no one else has, allowing him to trade ahead of the market.

So, if news is unpredictable and market performance reacts to news, then market performance is unpredictable.

Wait a minute. Are you saying then that all those Wall Street experts like Jim Cramer and Charles Paine really have no idea what they're talking about?

Yes...and No. They certainly know many things. But so do millions of other traders. Everything they know is already factored into a stock's price. It's what they don't know, the future news, which will drive stock prices. They are simply speculating as to what they think the news will be.

Sometimes they get it right...most of the time they get it wrong. Studies show that for the last 5 years, ending June 30, 2017, 82% of all U.S. large-cap mutual fund managers failed to beat their S&P 500 benchmark index over 5 years.[viii] Even worse, over the long term, the S&P 500 outperformed more than 92% of large-cap funds over the last 15 years.[ix]

The Law of Large Numbers

Imagine we fill the Soldier Field in Chicago with 20,000 people. On the PA system, we instruct them all to stand up and remove a quarter from their pocket.

On our mark, they all flip the coin. Those who flipped heads (about 10,000) remain standing. Those who flipped tails sit down. We now repeat this exercise, again and again. With 20,000 people flipping coins, we are willing to bet our houses that at least one person in the dome will flip heads ten straight times. In fact, we wouldn't be surprised if at least 20 people did it.

The law of large numbers states that if you have enough people try to do something, someone will succeed regardless of skill level. The individual who tossed heads 10 straight times...is he an expert coin flipper? Does he somehow understand the gravitational properties between his quarter, his wrist, and the earth? Or was he just lucky?

Guess how many publicly traded mutual funds, ETFs and UITs there are...19,215^{x} as of 2016. Someone is bound to speculate correctly on the market's reaction to news that has yet to occur.

The successful coin flipper is called lucky. The successful stock picker is called a guru and gets his face on magazines.

Again, we'll concede that these people are smart. Most went to the very best business schools in the country where they were taught that markets and stock prices are not predictable. But when they arrived on Wall Street, they were told how their firms really make money: trades.

Over 1 billion trades a month at $9 per trade on the New York Stock Exchange alone. You do the math. It is in *their* best interest to trade...not yours.

We do think that these very smart people honestly believe they have found a peek into the future. If there were only a handful of them researching companies, then they might actually be onto something. But there are thousands, all crunching the same data. Furthermore, their efforts to buy and sell ahead of the market incur costs that lower their rates of return.

In 2013, Eugene Fama won the Nobel Prize in economics for stating in the 1960's that something is worth only what someone is willing to pay for it. Called The Efficient Market Hypothesis, Fama showed (with a bunch of math) that the current price of stock or bond is the correct price. Nothing is overvalued or undervalued until someone offers or agrees to a different price.

If you buy a house for $300,000, spend $50,000 for improvement, and put it up for sale, how much is it worth if the highest offer you receive is $290,000?

Correct. It's worth $290,000.

So if it's true for real estate, why not stocks?

The $6 watch

Zach Norris is a young man with a passion for fine watches. Understanding that often people don't know the value of their old jewelry, he routinely visits thrift shops and garage sales looking for great deals. If he sees a watch that he knows he can quickly resell for a profit, he will buy it for the asking price and then quickly find a new buyer. In January of 2015, he bought a $6 watch at his local Goodwill store and then sold it for $35,000.

Norris is to watches what Wall Street portfolio managers aspire to be to stocks. But unlike Mr. Norris, they deal in public information. Had Goodwill known the watch was worth $35,000, would they have sold it for $6? Or, would the prior owner have given away the watch to Goodwill in the first place? Of course not. Mr. Norris had insider knowledge. In this case, he can legally act on it. But in the world of security trading, such a move can land you in jail (see Martha Stewart and Bud Fox).

Perhaps there was a time when news traveled slowly enough for someone to get a jump. Those days are over.

There is no Nostradamus. News occurs randomly, and so too will stock and bond prices. All we have going for us is that over the history of mankind, good news has outperformed bad. Despite world wars, famines, epidemics, assassinations, national debt, and disco, capitalism finds a way to improve the quality of life. The quality of your life today dwarfs that of every king and queen of the middle ages. It dwarfs that of your great grandparents, and even your grandparents. Is it not only logical to assume that in the future we will witness massive amounts of bad news but overall, we will prosper?

We don't need Nostradamus to conclude that optimistically is the realistic way to view the future. Hence, actions like market timing and stock picking are far less likely to succeed than buying, adjusting risk, and rebalancing a broadly diversified portfolio.

Don't just take our word for it (books to read)

The Investment Answer by Daniel Goldie and Gordon Murray

Random Walk Down Wall Street by Burton Malkeil

The Smartest Investment Book You'll Ever Own by Dan Solin

What Wall Street Doesn't Want You to Know by Larry Swedroe

Winning the Loser's Game by Charles Ellis

Your Math Teacher Was Right
(but you always knew that)

"Mathematics are well and good but nature keeps dragging us around by the nose. " – Albert Einstein

You remember Mrs. Cheeseman...the matronly math teacher who has been teaching out of the same book for thirty years because "the math hasn't changed. As you looked at the inside cover of the book, you saw the names and years of the prior holders. "Was it as boring for Fred Saddlemire in 1968 as it is for me now?" you asked yourself. "Was Mrs. Cheeseman ever cool?"

The one question that rose above all others was, "Will I ever need to know this stuff?"

Mrs. Cheeseman assured us we would. Now you're about to see at she was right.

Meet Hans & Franz. When not pumping iron and injecting themselves with steroids, they are drawing income from their savings accumulated from years on late night TV. Aside from an occasional State Farm commercial, the two are pretty much retired.

Convinced that no one should invest like a girlie man, Hans has invested heavily in equities under the belief that over time he stands to earn a higher rate of return. Chances are he'll be right.

Franz is no stranger to machismo, but opts for a portfolio that is likely to produce a lower, more consistent rate of return. Starting with one million each, they both desire to withdraw $50,000 per year to supplement their SNL royalty checks.

Hans and Franz are about to learn what Mrs. Cheeseman taught us years ago.

Average may not be as important as consistency of return.*

Hans: $1,000,000			
Year	Withdrawal	Return	Y/E Value
1	$50,000.00	-13	$826,500.00
2	$50,000.00	-20%	$661,200.00
3	$50,000.00	5%	$694,260.00
4	$50,000.00	-7%	$599,161.80
5	$50,000.00	20%	$658,994.16
6	$50,000.00	25%	$761,242.70
7	$50,000.00	-25%	$533,432.03
8	$50,000.00	45%	$700,976.44
9	$50,000.00	30%	$846,269.37
10	$50,000.00	20%	***$908,060.56***
Return Average: 8%			

Franz: $1,000,000			
Year	Withdrawal	Return	Y/E Value
1	$50,000.00	6%	$1,007,000.00
2	$50,000.00	8%	$1,087,560.00
3	$50,000.00	7%	$1,163,689.20
4	$50,000.00	11%	$1,236,195.01
5	$50,000.00	-4%	$1,138,747.21
6	$50,000.00	6%	$1,154,072.04
7	$50,000.00	12%	$1,236,560.69
8	$50,000.00	-2%	$1,162,829.48
9	$50,000.00	10%	$1,224,112.42
10	$50,000.00	6%	***$1,244,559.17***
Return Average: 6%			

*Returns are hypothetical and for illustration purposes only

As you can see, although Hans indeed earned a higher average return (8% vs. 6%) at the end of ten years, he has considerably less money than his body-building brother. Why? Every year, the two sell a part of their portfolios' shares to generate cash. When shares rise in value, it requires fewer shares to generate $50,000. When share prices fall, Hans must sell more. Those extra shares, once sold, are gone. It matters not what his portfolio does in the future in relation to those shares. He will never get them back

By minimizing his potential downside, Franz has more money even though he averaged less over time. Fewer negative years means he sells fewer shares.

This phenomenon exists only because Hans and Franz need to sell shares for cash. Had they never needed to sell shares, then Hans would have more much money than Franz, despite the volatility. This is the Math of Retirement.

Mrs. Cheeseman taught us that nothing in life performs consistently--not the weather, not your golf score, and certainly not an investment portfolio. This lack of consistency can be measured. It is called standard deviation. The lower the standard deviation, the more likely you will earn the average return each and every year. So, if you found a portfolio with a guaranteed return of 8% every year, then the standard deviation would be zero. Good luck finding that. Chances are, the best you'll do in seeking your 8% is a portfolio with a standard deviation of ten. So, what does that mean?

If Average Return is 8% and Standard Deviation is ten, then:

66% of the time: You will have a one year return between -2% and 18%.

95% of the time: You will have a one year return between -12% and 28%.

99% of the time: You will have a one year return between -22% and 38%.

*Returns are hypothetical and for illustration purposes only

If you are an investor, then your portfolio also has a long-term average return and a standard deviation to go along with it. The problem is that very few people know this, nor do they understand the "normal" volatility that comes with it. If they did, we think they'd be much less likely to panic.

For example, if a portfolio has the dimensions described in the chart above, should we be surprised (or even disappointed) if we earn a return of -6% in a given year?

Of course not. We already know going in that this is very likely. We also know that over time, it's more likely that we'll have more positive results than negative results. Guaranteed? No. Likely? Yes.

Think of it like baking a cake. You can put in the best ingredients, but you have soup unless you put the cake in the oven for the right amount of time.

Results do not come in a linear fashion, no matter how badly we wish they did. What in life does? Do the giant redwoods of northern California grow the same number of feet every year? Does it take you the same number of minutes to drive to work each day? Do farmers dig up their corn seeds every few days to see if they are sprouting, or have they learned to trust the process?

It is essential that you know the long-term average return and standard deviation of your portfolio allocation. Without knowing, you are simply winging it; and your survival mechanism stands a much better chance of over-riding your logic.

Know your math. Make Mrs. Cheeseman proud!

Don't just take our word for it (books to read):

The Intelligent Asset Allocator by William Bernstein

All About Asset Allocation by Richard Feri

Asset Allocation by Roger Gibson

The Boogeyman is Real

"The only two things that scare me are God and the IRS" –Dr. Dre

Assuming that you do not define patriotism by the amount you pay in tax, what follows should be useful. After all, even the IRS acknowledges that "Tax Avoidance is legal. Tax Evasion is illegal."

One of the most valuable benefits to my clients is that we have our own in-house tax practice, with a CPA and Enrolled Agent on staff, to compliment the financial advisory practice. The combination of the two allows us to be proactive in tax (avoidance) reduction strategies for clients. These strategies are not in the grey area, they are black and white and in existing tax code. Too few people take advantage and needlessly overpay thousands in taxes every year.

If you're one of the 55% of Americans who pay federal income taxes[xi], then it is likely you pay more than what is legally required. If you own a small business, then it's almost a sure thing that you are over paying.

The Seven Most Expensive Words in the English Language: My CPA takes care of my taxes.

From our experience, most CPAs do a great job of filing taxes; but very few actually do any tax real planning. When I ask people, when was the last time their CPA said he found a way to lower your taxes by $4,000, they usually give me a blank stare and then say, "Never."

Does your CPA/Tax Preparer ever:

- Call you with proactive strategies to achieve a tax-free retirement?

- Demonstrate how to restructure your 401k/403b/IRA accounts to avoid future taxation?

- How to collect your social security benefits TAX FREE?

- Show you how to structure your business to minimize employment taxes?

- Show you how to write off your family's medical bills as a business expense?

- Show you how you can hire children (or grandchildren) to shift income from yourself to them?

- Help you choose the right retirement plan for your business?

- Explain how each of your investments is taxed and make suggestions on how to reduce it?

- Advise you on how to carefully consider which investments belong in taxable accounts and which investments belong in tax-advantaged accounts?

- Develop a plan for maximizing the value of any long-term capital loss carryforwards?

- Explain the rules governing "passive" income and losses and have a plan to avoid "suspended" losses?

- Meet with you throughout the year to discuss your business--or does he just wait until taxes are due?

- Give you a plan for minimizing taxes-- or does he/she just wing it every year?

Aside from investing behavior, income taxes are the greatest obstacle to most investors. There is never an age at which you stop paying them. You paid tax on your social security as you put money into the system, and you will likely pay tax on the money as it comes out.

When you reach age 70.5, you must start paying tax on your retirement plans (401k, IRA, 403b). When you die, your heirs must also pay tax on whatever is left.

Your estate may be taxed again for simply being too big or improperly planned.

The tax code is, by design, very complicated.

Too often, people just go along with it, unaware of the steps that can legally reduce their federal and state income taxes. This is especially important during retirement.

You have a choice of paying taxes now...or later. To many, procrastination seems logical when it comes paying the IRS. For years people have socked away massive amounts of money in 401ks, 403bs, IRAs. The idea is you invest it now in a tax deductible account while you're in a high tax bracket. Then you withdraw it at a lower tax bracket when you retire. Or so you hope.

What if taxes rise in the future? Our country, as of 2017, owes more than $20 trillion[xii]. Projections suggest this amount will continue to rise as more and more baby boomers retire. Fewer people paying taxes and more requiring things like Medicare, Medicaid, and Social Security.

Despite the recent Trump Tax Bill claiming to reduce taxes, after kicking the can down the road for two decades, eventually someone has to pay for all the government debt and taxes have to go up. Maybe this is why the individual tax cuts were temporary. We have financed the economic recovery 2000-2017 with zero interest rates and borrowing from the future to pay for today.

Case Study

Bill & Karen Tucker are both 65. Retired, they each have a rollover IRA worth $600,000. Bill collects $2,200 a month from social security. Karen receives $1,800. They need $7,000 a month to live comfortably, so they withdraw $3,000 a month from their retirement accounts. To determine how much of their social security check is subject to taxation, we add the IRA withdrawals ($36,000) to one-half of the social security payments ($24,000) This gives them a modified adjust gross income (MAGI) of $60,000. Whenever the MAGI exceeds $44,000 for a married couple, then up to 85% of their check is subjected to taxation.

Assuming they file jointly and use the standard deduction, Bill & Karen owe $4,300 in Federal income taxes. Now, what if they had decided a few years back to convert their rollover IRAs to a Roth IRA? Doing so would have triggered at the time of conversion, but no tax would ever be owned on the accounts again. Even if their accounts double in value, there is no tax associated with a Roth withdrawal. Not only is there no tax on Roth IRA withdrawals, but now there would also be no tax owed on their Social Security benefits. Furthermore, Bill & Karen could now withdraw an additional $16,400 from their taxable IRA and still pay $0 in tax since they still have their standard deduction and exemption to apply.

Imagine if federal income tax rates double in the future. By converting to a Roth, the Tucker's have protected themselves.

Another tax advantaged vehicle is permanent life insurance. Money in the policy grows tax deferred and can be accessed tax free via a policy loan. While I don't usually recommend retirees buy life insurance, this feature is a great reason to keep your policy even after you've stopped working.

Like a lot of people we meet, the Tuckers rely solely on their accountant for tax advice. But from our experience, many accountants work as tax filers, not tax planners.

Tax planning is one of the most ignored areas of financial planning, and failure to address IRS lien on savings is ruining people. It is not the job of the IRS to tell you how to lower your taxes. It's your job. If you don't know how, you need to find a professional who does. You won't find him inside a box of turbo tax software.

The tax code is very complicated. Too often people just go along with it, unaware of the steps that can legally reduce their federal and state income taxes. Failure to address this issue can mean you're not worth anywhere close to what you think.

If you want to know more about real tax planning, we'll show you how we use our Tax Blueprint™ to rescue retirement plans for our clients.

Don't just take our word for it (books to read):

How to Pay Zero Taxes 2016 by J.K. Lasser

The Power of Zero by David McKnight

It Will Probably End Badly

"It's paradoxical, that the idea of living a long life appeals to everyone, but the idea of getting old doesn't appeal to anyone."

— Andy Rooney

An earlier chapter ended with a statement that the future is always likely to be better than the past. For society as a whole, we truly believe that. As for our individual lives, we know that life is finite. The Grim Reaper is undefeated. And while modern medicine has made huge strides in fighting heart disease, diabetes, and cancer, we all still die.

The lucky ones will die suddenly, like Tim Russert. Here today living life to the fullest...gone tomorrow. Sad for our loved ones, but much better than dying a slow death where our health declines daily, limited to a wheelchair, incapable of recalling our children's names, and needing assistance to visit the bathroom.

Depressing...isn't it? That's life.

As a society, we are living longer. That is a good thing, but that also means our money must last longer. It means that eventually we will become weak and likely to need help with those things we only want to do for ourselves (custodial care).

Some stats from the National Institute for Health[xiii]:

- If you reach age 65, there's a 70% chance you'll need custodial care.
- The average nursing home stay is almost three years.
- The average private room nursing home cost is $83,585 a year.
- Less than 20% of older people have enough resources to live in a nursing home for more than 3 years.
- Medicare doesn't pay for Long Term Care.

- Medicaid is available only after you've spent down your assets.
- Most people in nursing homes are on Medicaid, but they didn't start there.

Basically, you have three options when it comes to long term care.

- First, you can self-insure the exposure. Perhaps you have enough money to do just that. Remember...average cost is $83,585[xiv]. At 6% inflation, the price will double in twelve years. If you're married and you get sick, will that leave enough money for your healthy spouse?

- Second, you can rely on Medicaid. Why not? Most do, but, that's available only after you've spent down your own money. If you're married, Medicaid kicks in when you have about $100,000 left. You don't have to sell your house, but the government may attach a lien to it after you die so that it can recoup the cost of your care.

- Third, you can buy long term care insurance or a long term care hybrid life insurance combo (which costs are capped and has a death benefit). For many people, this is the right choice. Often, we hear people say they won't buy it out of fear they'll never use it, and thus waste their money. We're going to let you in on a little secret: the people who go to nursing homes with long term care don't win the game. It's those who have long term care insurance but die peacefully in their sleep, healthy today...dead tomorrow, who win the game.

When your car isn't stolen, do you regret owing auto insurance? Never feel regret for being prudent.

Long term care insurance can be expensive, but a few things can be done to reduce it:

1. Limit coverage to four years. Odds are very high you won't need the policy after four years. By limiting coverage to four years, you reduce the cost dramatically over a lifetime benefit policy.

2. Self-insure a part of the cost. If nursing homes in your area cost $200 per day, consider coverage for $150. Be sure to study the long term impact of not being fully insured.

3. Buy a long term care life insurance hybrid. It provides a fixed cost, unlike traditional long term care insurance and if you don't use it, there is a death benefit of what you paid in.

Whatever you do...have a plan! It's not a matter of if, but when!

Don't just take our word for it: Long Term Care: <u>Your Financial Planning Guide</u> by Phyllis Shelton

Your Brain is Messed Up

"We have seen the enemy, and he is us."

—Pogo

Perhaps the biggest obstacle (no, not *perhaps*...it really *is* the biggest) toward financial success is our own brain...our humanness...our emotions.

God gave us many gifts; but if misused, they can be self-destructive.

Consider weight loss. Technically, losing weight is very easy. We simply exercise more and eat less. Yet, we are the fattest nation on earth; and weight loss is a multi-billion dollar industry. Why?

Investing is also quite simple: buy when prices are low. Sell when they are high. According to the Dalbar study, we see that simple strategy ignored all the time. People often do the complete opposite.

Let's take Marty McFly's time traveling Delorean back a few years....to 10,000 BC.

Meet your great, great, great, great, great, great, great, great, great (you get the idea) grandfather. We'll call him Fred. He lives in a cave with his mate Wilma and their children Pebbles and Bam Bam (whom they adopted after a T-Rex ate Barney & Betty Rubble).

Life is very simple for Fred and Wilma. Fred wakes up, sharpens his spear, and kills whatever he can find. He brings it back to the cave where Wilma cooks it.

Fred is motivated to stop the pains of hunger, cold, and predators. He seeks warmth and comfort where he can; but above all else, he tries to avoid pain for his family and himself. He doesn't know it, but Fred has within his brain a survival mechanism that motivates him to behave this way. It is his natural tendency to flee from danger. In fact, all animals have it--

another gift from God. Fred doesn't worry about his cholesterol level, his A1C results, or his blood pressure. He merely wants to stay fed, warm, and safe. Fred was the original couch potato whenever the opportunity presented itself.

Food, water, safety, and warmth...that's all he thinks about. Morality, personal fulfillment, spirituality....these don't matter to him at all. It's a struggle just to meet the basics.

Fast forward to present day. We don't have Fred's worries. Far from it. Food? In the US, a major health problem amongst our poor is obesity. Water, warmth...readily available. The survival mechanism that kept Fred alive until a sabretooth tiger ate him is still present in our brains. We don't use it often, but it's there...lurking.

Need to lose weight by eating less (painful) and exercising (even more painful). Forget it. Our brain tells us we're crazy. Stay in bed. Rest. Relax.

Fred didn't care if he lived past age 40, but you do. Rather than helping you though, the survival mechanism is betraying you.

When your stocks fall in value, you experience pain. Your brain tells you that you must do something. You must sell. When what you sold starts increasing in value, you feel worse! You know logically that stocks are likely to rebound, but your brain convinces you that "this time is different."

While the survival mechanism is the worse feature of our psyche when it comes to investing, there are a few others that can be equally destructive:

Herding: When we were teenaged, we called it "peer pressure". Our mothers asked, "If Johnny told you to jump off a bridge, would you?" Hey, bridge jumping can be great fun.

When Frank in accounting tells you that everyone is dumping the index fund in the company 401k and loading up heavily on company stock, you need to remind yourself of something. Unless Frank is having secret meetings with the company chairman, he knows nothing more than the rest of the world. All the information about your company is already factored into its stock. Frank is just speculating. Sadly, there were several "Franks" working at Enron.

Confirmation Bias: We'd all like to believe that we are objective thinkers, weighing all facts before making a decision or establishing a belief. Sorry...not true. There are things we WANT to believe are true. So much so, we'll ignore any evidence to the contrary. Take Nikki's daughter, Georgie. At age 8, she is committed to believing in Santa Clause. She's heard from classmates that St. Nick isn't real, but every year she finds evidence to the contrary (thanks to her mom). In her mind, the kids who don't believe are simply the ones who misbehave and receive nothing on December 25th.

For other people, we see confirmation bias in areas like climate change, the Kennedy assassination, or the future price of gold.

In 2001, I met a GE engineer who said he had no intention of ever diversifying away from his company stock. "I don't want to hear it," he said to us when we suggested a broader allocation. He was 64, and the stock comprised 100% of his portfolio. In the previous ten years, his net worth had tripled. It seemed invincible.

At that point, the stock was trading at $65 a share. Seven years later, it was worth $8. In 2017, it's worth less than $20.

When it comes to matters of finance, confirmation bias can be expensive.

Gambler's Fallacy: The roulette wheel has come up red the last six times. It must turn up black this time, right? No wait...six times in a row? It has to turn up red a seventh time. It's on a roll.

Of course, both statements are false. The Gambler believes that despite randomness, past events influence further events. This is why casinos give free hotel rooms to high rollers. Just don't leave our casino. We know eventually you will give the money back. You'll believe you have skill, but we know it is pure chance...and the odds of chance favor the house.

We see it with stocks all the time. The market is up, and "experts" call for a "correction". In order for there to be a correction, we must first have a mistake. The "correction assumption" is that stocks are mispriced. Eventually the market will wake up this reality, causing prices to adjust.

It's hogwash. News drives stock prices. Markets will move randomly because news occurs randomly.

Anchoring: Back to our GE engineer. His wife saw the potential mistake of holding just one stock, but even she couldn't be swayed toward logic because they knew diversification would trigger taxation. So anchored was she in her belief that taxes are bad, she put herself in a position of eventually owing no tax because they lost most of their portfolio in 2008. Oh, to have Marty's Delorean.

A successful investor understands that logic doesn't come naturally. He seeks out ways to ensure that when it comes to money, the left side of his brain stays in control.

Don't just take our word for it (books to read):

Predictably Irrational by Dan Ariely

The Behavior Gap by Carl Richards

Rick Perry Was Right

"The real sin with Social Security is that it's a long-term rip-off and a short-term scam."
                                           —*Tony Snow*

A Ponzi scheme is an investment fraud that involves the payment of purported returns to existing investors from funds contributed by new investors. Ponzi scheme organizers often solicit new investors by promising to invest funds in opportunities claimed to generate high returns with little or no risk. In many Ponzi schemes, the fraudsters focus on attracting new money to make promised payments to earlier-stage investors to create the false appearance that investors are profiting from a legitimate business.

With little or no legitimate earnings, Ponzi schemes require a consistent flow of money from new investors to continue. Ponzi schemes tend to collapse when it becomes difficult to recruit new investors or when a large number of investors ask to cash out.

--United States Securities & Exchange Commission[xv]

In the 2012 election primary, pundits attacked Texas Governor Rick Perry for correctly describing the Social Security system as a Ponzi scheme. The system, which began in 1940, then taxed 159 workers for every 1 retiree a maximum total of $30 per year. Today, it taxes 2.8 workers for every 1 retiree 6.2% of their earnings (up to $118,550)[xvi]. If you're self-employed, you pay the tax twice.

Money is taken from workers and is transferred to retirees. The rate of return is not guaranteed. Most people will average between two and four percent. Many will lose money if they die before they receive benefits equal to their contributions. Unlike your savings, you cannot leave your social security benefits to your children. At least Charles Ponzi gave some investors a high rate of return.

Social Security today is not what it was intended to be when President Roosevelt signed the program into existence in 1935. Its original intent was to aid Americans who couldn't take care of themselves, such as widows and orphans. It was never designed to be the sole means for retirement income, which it has become for many Americans today.

In 1940, life expectancy was 61 for men and 65 for women[xvii]; while the earliest one could collect benefits back then was age 65. On average, you were more likely to die than receive long-term benefits. Ironically, one of the very first people to receive a check, Ida May Fuller, lived to be 100 years old. These days about 62 million people receive benefits in excess of $955 billion[xviii].

Benefit Timing

For many retirees, the question of when to take benefits can be a difficult one. The longer you wait to start collecting, the larger your monthly check. Full retirement age is between 65 and 67 depending on what year you were born.

You can take benefits as early as 62, but receive 25% less per month than if you hold out until your full retirement age. If you wait until age 70 to collect, then you get 32% more. In real dollars that means if your full retirement benefit is $2,000 but you elected to take it at 62, you will receive $1,500 each month. Likewise, if you wait until age 70, you will receive $2,700 every month.

Life expectancy plays a major role in determining the timing of your social security benefits. The breakeven point for taking benefits at 62 vs. 70 is age 78.

If you had that time machine and knew your expiration date – no problem. Of course if you delay taking your benefit, it may mean you have to spend more of your savings in the early years of retirement.

Many factors need to be taken into consideration when taking social security. Our firm has invested in software that takes your specific circumstances in to account and produces the "What if's?" and we provide this detail in a free Social Security timing report to ensure that you make the right choices for your family in an attempt to maximize your lifetime social security benefits.

So what is the future of Social Security? Is it sustainable? What was once a 1% tax is now 6.2%. As fewer people pay in and more are recipients, the percentage could always be increased. The amount of income subject to the tax could be increased, and inflationary increases could be eliminated or decreased. Lots of appealing options...

No political party wants to broach the elimination of Social Security, and they likely won't. Social Security in its current state isn't at all what Roosevelt had in mind in 1935, so change is always a strong possibility.

Don't Just Take Our Word For It:

 Get What's Yours: The Secrets to Maxing Out Your Social Security by Laurence J. Kotlikoff, Phillip Moeller and Paul Solman

---

Flat Abs, Low Cholesterol, and Wealth

To get these, you probably need help

"Everyone needs a coach. It doesn't matter whether you're a basketball player, a tennis player, a gymnast or a bridge player."

--Bill Gates

At age 51, he finally got the news: "Dan, you're fat, your blood sugar is too high, and so is your blood pressure. Other than that, you're doing great...for a 70 year old."

He couldn't argue with the doctor. Everything he said was true.

"If you're serious about this, I can coach you through it," he said. "Every three months, going forward, you'll come in for new blood work and a review of your eating habits for the past three months. In addition, you'll spend time with my nutritionist. Lastly, you will hire a personal trainer who will give you a full body workout three times a week."

Three months later, Dan lost 15 pounds, and blood sugar level (A1C) dropped from 7.1 to 5.7 (you want it below 6.5).

Could he have done it without the nutritionist and trainer? Technically, yes. Realistically, not a chance. When the alarm goes off at 5:30 a.m., he now jumps out of bed because the trainer awaits him at the gym. If it were up to Dan to work out alone, that alarm would never be set. He admits he would just procrastinate. When he did get around to exercising, it would be with half the intensity his trainer demands. Why? Because exercise is painful. Sleep is pleasurable. Steel cut oatmeal doesn't taste nearly as good as a Dunkin' Donut.

On our own, we rarely perform at our optimal level. A good coach will not only help achieve excellence, he'll assist in keeping us there.

A good coach sees things we can't (or don't want to see).

He forces us to leave our comfort zone and to apply logic when emotion is in overdrive. He holds us accountable to ourselves.

One of the biggest failings in the financial services industry is the failure to understand this. The industry is dominated not by coaches (or even advisors) but by commission salesmen. They push product as the answer and then go looking for the question. Objectivity is lost, and the client pays the price.

A good wealth coach services his client with a holistic approach and commits himself to putting the needs of the client first.

Over nearly 20 years, Dan and Mike have refined our process to offer such a service. It's a four-step process called The Wealth Coaching Program.

Step One: The Consultation-- We begin every first meeting with a simple question:

"What will make this a great meeting for you today?" We want the client to set the agenda. More importantly, we want to know what keeps them up at night.

If on a scale of one to ten (ten means you sleep like Bill Gates, and one means you don't sleep at all), how do you rate your financial situation? If you are a nine or a ten, you're done. Give this book to a friend, and go live your life. No need for any coaching. You are Tiger Woods in 2000.

But if you are more like a seven (or lower), then what has to occur for you to be a ten, aside from winning the lottery? We find that it's rarely about the amount of money one has. The most anxious people we've ever met had significant wealth. Despite that, they were fearful, frustrated, and even angry. In some cases, they were victimized by other advisors. To get most people to a ten, it takes a strategy that they have a hand in designing. They require a plan that details fully the pros and cons, and is simple enough that they can explain it to a friend.

Do you need to be a financial expert to be a ten? No. Just like we don't need to know how a hybrid engine works to drive a car. We do need to know how to start the car (which if you haven't bought a car lately, isn't as easy as it used to be). We need to know how to put the car in gear, and how to turn the wheel. We need to know when gas is needed, when to rotate the tires, and when to change the oil. Simple stuff, but it is required.

A well designed financial strategy answers questions like:

1. How much can I spend during retirement without a strong chance of going broke?

2. What rate of return do I really need on my money, and how can I get it with the least amount of volatility?

3. How can I protect myself from speculation (stock picking, market timing)?

4. How will I deal with catastrophe, such as failing health?

5. How can I legally pay the IRS less?

6. How can I most efficiently transfer my assets at death?

Step Two: The Creation-- Then questions to step one are answered by making you part of the plan's design. A good coach listens to what you want to accomplish (I want $X a month for life, after tax, indexed for inflation) and then offers the pros and cons of achieving that goal. And trust me...there are always cons. Lots of them. You need to know them.

Together we draw up the plan.

How much of your income do you want guaranteed? Before you say "all of it," know that guaranteed usually comes with two costs: low return and less for your heirs.

If you choose to have some or all of your money in a non-guaranteed portfolio, do you fully understand the likely range of returns? What is your worst year likely to be (statistically)?   And when it happens (and it will), what will you do?

How much (if any) would you like to leave your children?

How do you wish to handle the cost of custodial care should you need it (and you probably will)?

If you choose to make no changes, what are your chances for success? Are you okay with that?

Step Three: The Consideration--Only after the design is fully complete can the plan be written. Back when Dan's blood results showed he had too much sugar in his blood, he and his doctor together discussed the ups and downs of the strategy: costs, time, denial of certain foods, etc. Once that was outlined, then they actually created a written plan.

Medications can be used to fight illness. The doctor doesn't care where you fill the prescription. He simply wants you to fully take the meds.

In personal finance, products are the medication. While a coach can assist you in acquiring them, it should not be a requirement for being coached. Sadly, we too often see financial advisors offer "free" planning. There is no such thing as free. You will pay for it, one way or another. Typically, the "plan" is nothing more than a sales proposal to buy product. "We'll give you a free plan that will recommend you buy a commission-based product from us."

At our firm, we charge for the financial plan, if you implement through us we will credit the planning fee. If you do not want to implement through us, that's OK, but we still get paid by you for providing a comprehensive financial plan based on your goals.

In addition to delivering the written plan, we provide the client with a list of recommendations on a single page. With each recommendation, we ask a few simple questions:

1. Do you fully understand this recommendation? Do you know the pros and cons?

2. Are you going to implement it (yes or no...never a "let me think about it")?

3. How are you going to implement it? Are you going work with someone (insurance agent, investment advisor)?

No loose ends.

Step Four: The Coaching & Education Stage-- Our firm educates our clients in groups, but coaches them one on one. Some of the education classes many times reiterate important concepts that are helpful in understanding the long-term issues facing retirement. Other classes delve deeper into the client's emotions. Almost all of our decisions are emotion based. We need to accept and understand that. By being in tune with our values, we are much more likely to reach a purpose for our money that reflects these values.

Final Thoughts

When our parents and grandparents retired, life was much simpler. At 65 they took Social Security and hopefully they had a pension from a long-time job with a gold watch at retirement.

Those days are gone.

Today, pensions have gone the way of the Do-Do Bird. Social Security is a complex maze of take it at 62-66-67-70 and don't forget how those choices will impact not only your benefit, but the benefits available to your spouse, surviving spouse and potentially children.

Every man, woman and child is responsible for self-funding their retirement through 401ks, 403bs, 457 plans, Traditional IRAs, Roth IRAs, Life Insurance etc... The unfortunate thing is that as the government and business policies have made individuals responsible, they have not provided the basic education on what it takes to be successful. In fact, they conceal the facts to ensure that you have to come to them.

Wall Street salesman complicate matters even more by pushing products to generate revenue for their firms and commissions for themselves, long before it's determined what you actually need.

That's really the theme and take away from this book of Lessons Learned...what do YOU need?

What does a successful retirement look like to you and your spouse? How much income will you need? What will you do in retirement? Do you want to leave a legacy for the kids, grandkids or church? Do you have a plan for reducing your taxes?

Notice, none of these questions were about investments, mutual funds, annuities, bonds, stocks or rates of return. They were about what YOU need- the Purpose- not how do we get the most Performance.

Only by answering the initial questions can a financial doctor then prescribe a solution – the appropriate mix of investments right for you based on your goals.

Retirement is not about accumulation
Retirement is about distributions

The same things that got you here, throw money at the market and hope it goes up over the next 30 years, are not the same things that will make you successful in retirement. If you're over 50, you no longer have 5-10 years to take a big portfolio loss and wait to break even at some point in the future.

If you're like many of my clients that are in or approaching retirement, they are looking for conservative solutions that will ensure that the focus remains on retirement income and low volatility portfolios.

At this stage of life, you've saved and sacrificed to get here, you're at the goal line. With proper planning, you've won the game. The goal here is to not screw it up by taking too much risk or leaving too much to chance.

I will end asking the most important question that you must ask yourself;

"If you had enough income in retirement to do all the things you wanted to do, would you care about account balances or market ups and downs?" No, it's all about generating income. In retirement, growth is important, but it is secondary to a reliable income generating portfolio that you can't outlive.

I wish you well in your pursuit of independence and dignity in retirement.

Never forget that it's what you've worked your entire life for.

About the Author: Michael Stewart, MBA, RFC

Michael Stewart is the Managing Partner of Crystal Lake Tax & Financial, a financial and tax planning firm located in Crystal Lake, Illinois. Michael holds degrees from both Creighton University and American University.

As a financial planner, he also holds the designation of Registered Financial Consultant and has earned a Certificate in Financial Planning through the American College.

His firm is fee-based and works with over 200 families throughout the United States on conservative income-based planning.

Mike and his wife Karen live in McHenry, Illinois.

Investment Advisory Services offered through Sound Income Strategies, LLC, an SEC Registered Investment Advisory Firm. Crystal Lake Tax & Financial and Sound Income Strategies, LLC are not associated entities.

About the Author: Dan Cuprill, CFP

Dan Cuprill is the president of Matson & Cuprill, a wealth coaching and advisory firm located in Cincinnati, Ohio. A graduate of the University of Iowa & Northwestern University, his fee-based firm works with over 200 families in 20 states. He has been featured in USA Today, The Wall Street Journal, and the Cincinnati Enquirer among other media outlets.

A Certified Financial Planner, he also holds the Chartered Life Underwriter and Chartered Financial Advisor designations through the American College.

He and his wife Beth live in Loveland, Ohio.

Chapter Contributions by Author

Michael Stewart, MBA, RFC

> Introduction
>
> Purpose vs Performance
>
> Eat the Eggs, Not the Chickens
>
> The Boogeyman is Real
>
> Flat Abs, Low Cholesterol and Wealth
>
> Final Thoughts

Dan Cuprill, CFP

> There is No Nostradamus
>
> Your Math Teacher Was Right
>
> It Will Probably End Badly
>
> Your Brain is Messed Up
>
> Rick Perry Was Right
>
> Flat Abs, Low Cholesterol and Wealth

Disclosure

Important Note –

Crystal Lake Tax & Financial believes that education is a key step toward addressing your financial goals, and this material is designed to serve simply as an informational and educational resource.

Accordingly, this material does not offer or constitute investment advice and makes no direct or indirect recommendation of any particular product or of the appropriateness of any particular investment-related option.

Nothing in this book should be interpreted to state or imply that past results are an indication of future performance.

Investing involves substantial risk. Your needs, goals, and circumstances are unique, and they require the individualized attention of your financial professional.

End Notes & Citations

[i] http://www.macrotrends.net/2324/sp-500-historical-chart-data

[ii] https://upfina.com/bull-vs-bear-market/

[iii] https://www.csmonitor.com/Business/2013/0504/Bull-markets-how-this-one-stacks-up-in-history/1987-2000-582-percent-gain

[iv] https://www.fool.com/investing/general/2013/08/30/15-biases-that-make-you-do-dumb-things-with-your-m.aspx

[v] http://www.simplestockinvesting.com/SP500-historical-real-total-returns.htm

[vi]https://www.advisorperspectives.com/dshort/updates/2018/02/01/a-perspective-on-secular-bull-and-bear-markets

[vii] https://www.statista.com/statistics/261713/changes-of-the-sundp-500-during-the-us-election-years-since-1928/

[viii] http://us.spindices.com/spiva/#/reports

[ix] http://fortune.com/2017/04/13/stock-indexes-beat-mutual-funds/

[x] https://www.ici.org/pdf/2017_factbook.pdf

[xi] https://nypost.com/2017/04/18/almost-half-of-americans-wont-pay-federal-income-tax/

[xii] http://www.usdebtclock.org/

[xiii]https://www.census.gov/content/dam/Census/library/publications/2014/demo/p23-212.pdf

[xiv]https://www.census.gov/content/dam/Census/library/publications/2014/demo/p23-212.pdf

[xv] https://www.sec.gov/fast-answers/answersponzihtm.html

xvi https://www.ssa.gov/history/ratios.html

xvii http://www.demog.berkeley.edu/~andrew/1918/figure2.html

xviii https://www.ssa.gov/news/press/factsheets/basicfact-alt.pdf

Made in USA - Kendallville, IN
13142_9781983411472
02.24.2022 1435